THE TEN COMMANDMENTS

THE TEN COMMANDMENTS

Craig Munro

RITCHIE

John Ritchie Publishing

40 Beansburn, Kilmarnock, Scotland

ISBN-13: 978 1 912522 21 7

Copyright © 2018 by John Ritchie Ltd.
40 Beansburn, Kilmarnock, Scotland

www.ritchiechristianmedia.co.uk

Typeset by John Ritchie Ltd., Kilmarnock
Printed by Bell & Bain Ltd., Glasgow

Contents

Foreword

Modern books which deal specifically with the Ten Commandments are rare, so this new volume from the pen of Craig Munro is to be welcomed. Craig is very much aware of the teaching of the Epistle to the Romans that law-keeping has played no part in our justification; "a man is justified by faith without the deeds of the law" (ch.3.28). Neither does it contribute to our sanctification, for as believers "we have been discharged from the law, having died to that wherein we were holden; so that we serve in newness of the spirit, and not in oldness of the letter" (ch.7.6 RV). However, he contends that the basic moral principles of the law should be worked out in the lives of believers today in the power of the Holy Spirit (Romans 8.4).

He demonstrates that divine principles have never altered with the passing of the centuries, and so these commandments are still relevant for modern life. He shows the ramifications of God's law as it relates to our responsibilities to Him and to mankind around us, exploring the different ways in which it applies to life in the home, in the workplace and in the assembly.

Frequently, he draws attention to Him Who is the great exemplar of each of the tenets of God's law. The Lord Jesus exhibited fully and perpetually all that God demanded in these holy commands, the One "who did no sin" (1 Peter 2.22).

The reader will find great benefit in following through the many Bible references, as Old and New Testaments are cited extensively to back up relevant points either by clear statements or by way of illustration. The author's extensive knowledge of Scripture becomes obvious as he pulls in appropriate citations from what would sometimes be regarded as obscure areas of the Word.

Pondering this volume will encourage you to be like the "blessed" man of Psalm 1, whose "delight is in the law of the Lord" (v.2).

Jack Hay

Introduction

Reading, meditating, and obeying the Holy Scriptures are essential parts of a Christian's life. This book considers a portion of Exodus 20, where God first gives the Ten Commandments. It is probably the best 'known about' part of the Bible and it is often referenced in common day speech, even by people with a very limited understanding of the Bible. Perhaps, however, it is an area that is rarely explained and often misunderstood even amongst true believers. What place does 'the law' have for the Christian today? Do the Ten Commandments have any purpose for us now?

God willing, this book will be the start of a series of books dealing with a key chapter or section of Scripture. Initially, the intention is to publish accessible books on the following key chapters of the Bible in a descending numerical scale, for ready reference. For example:

1. The 10 Commandments - Exodus 20
2. The 9 Beatitudes - Matthew 5
3. The 8 Kingdom Parables - Matthew 13
4. The 7 Feasts of Jehovah - Leviticus 23
5. The 6 Days of Creation - Genesis 1

Each verse, commandment, beatitude, parable, feast, and day will be expounded briefly and the chapter will be readable in less than five minutes. At the end of each chapter is a space for notes. Readers can use this book as part of their daily reading and reflection and perhaps for group/Bible Class discussion.

All Scripture references will be placed in a footnote. The purpose is to allow each chapter to be read quickly, but to convince the reader that the argument presented is Scriptural, the references are normally quoted in full if they are not already quoted in the general text. I strongly encourage the reader to read these Scriptures. It is the Scriptures that carry the power to transform our lives.

The substance of this book was first published in the *Present Truth* magazine. The material has now been edited further and added to for this current volume. My simple prayer is that through the publishing of this book, the Lord Jesus may be exalted and God's people built up in their most holy faith. My burden is for a movement in our day back to the Bible with a deeper reverence and obedience to His Word.

Notes

Notes

Overview

Precepts

The Ten Commandments were given to Moses in Mount Sinai upon two tables of stone[1] and were written with the very finger of God[2]. They are found in Exodus 20.1-17 and in Deuteronomy 5.6-21:

Ex 20.1 *And God spake all these words, saying,*

Ex 20.2 *I am the LORD thy God, which have brought thee out of the land of Egypt, out of the house of bondage.*

First Commandment: *Ex 20.3 Thou shalt have no other gods before me.*

Second Commandment: *Ex 20.4 Thou shalt not make unto thee any graven image, or any likeness of any thing that is in heaven above, or that is in the earth beneath, or that is in the water under the earth:*

---

[1]Exodus 31.18: "And he gave unto Moses, when he had made an end of communing with him upon mount Sinai, two tables of testimony, tables of stone, written with the finger of God."

[2]Deuteronomy 9.10: "And the LORD delivered unto me two tables **of stone written with the finger of God; and on them** *was written according to all the words, which the LORD spake with you in the mount* out **of the midst of the fire in the day of the assembly."**

13

Ex 20.5 Thou shalt not bow down thyself to them, nor serve them: for I the LORD thy God am a jealous God, visiting the iniquity of the fathers upon the children unto the third and fourth generation of them that hate me;

Ex 20.6 And shewing mercy unto thousands of them that love me, and keep my commandments.

Third Commandment: *Ex 20.7 **Thou shalt not take the name of the LORD thy God in vain**; for the LORD will not hold him guiltless that taketh his name in vain.*

Fourth Commandment: *Ex 20.8 **Remember the sabbath day, to keep it holy.***

Ex 20.9 Six days shalt thou labour, and do all thy work:

Ex 20.10 But the seventh day is the sabbath of the LORD thy God: in it thou shalt not do any work, thou, nor thy son, nor thy daughter, thy manservant, nor thy maidservant, nor thy cattle, nor thy stranger that is within thy gates:

Ex 20.11 For in six days the LORD made heaven and earth, the sea, and all that in them is, and rested the seventh day: wherefore the LORD blessed the sabbath day, and hallowed it.

Fifth Commandment: *Ex 20.12 **Honour thy father and thy mother**: that thy days may be long upon the land which the LORD thy God giveth thee.*

Sixth Commandment: *Ex 20.13 **Thou shalt not kill.***

Seventh Commandment: *Ex 20.14 **Thou shalt not commit adultery.***

Eighth Commandment: *Ex 20.15 **Thou shalt not steal.***

Ninth Commandment: *Ex 20.16* ***Thou shalt not bear false witness against thy neighbour.***

Tenth Commandment: *Ex 20.17* ***Thou shalt not covet*** *thy neighbour's house, thou shalt not covet thy neighbour's wife, nor his manservant, nor his maidservant, nor his ox, nor his ass, nor any thing that is thy neighbour's.*

Principles
The first five commandments relate to our responsibilities toward God and emphasise many attributes of God and principles that are essential in our relationship with God.

Commandment 1
Thou shalt have no other gods before Me
Attribute: Solitariness of God
Principle: Response to the Uniqueness of God

Commandment 2
Thou shalt not make any graven image
Attribute: Supremacy of God
Principle: Recognition of the Jealousy of God

Commandment 3
Thou shalt not take the Name of the Lord thy God in vain
Attribute: Sovereignty of God
Principle: Reverence for the Name of God

Commandment 4
Remember the Sabbath day to keep it Holy
Attribute: Sanctity of God
Principle: Respect for the Rest of God

Commandment 5

Honour thy Father and Mother

Attribute: Stability of God

Principle: Regard for the Order of God

The second set of five commandments relates to our responsibilities towards people and stress principles that are essential for harmonious human relationships and values for life.

Commandment 6

Thou shalt not kill

Principle: Respect for life

Value: Life

Commandment 7

Thou shalt not commit adultery

Principle: Respect for marriage

Value: Purity

Commandment 8

Thou shalt not steal

Principle: Respect for another's belongings

Value: Honesty

Commandment 9

Thou shalt not bear false witness

Principle: Respect for truth

Value: Trust

Commandment 10

Thou shalt not covet

Principle: Respect for what I have

Value: Contentment

Purposes

The Ten Commandments (ten words) are part of 'the law', given by God in the first five books of the Bible. We shall show that the primary purpose for the giving of the law was to reveal Christ, to expose and highlight sin, emphasising to us our need of a Saviour, and to give principles through which, by the saving power and help of the Holy Spirit, we can live in harmony with God and each other.

1. The Law reveals the supreme glory of Christ

It was the Lord Jesus who showed that the books of Moses revealed Him: *"And beginning at Moses and all the prophets, he expounded unto them in all the scriptures the things concerning himself"*[3]; and again, *"He said unto them, These are the words which I spake unto you, while I was yet with you, that all things must be fulfilled, which were written in the law of Moses, and in the prophets, and in the psalms, concerning me. Then opened he their understanding, that they might understand the scriptures"*[4].

The fundamental lesson is, therefore, that we should read the Ten Commandments to see the glory of Christ.

2. The Law exposes sin and judgment

The Ten Commandments are largely given in the negative. Eight of them start: 'Thou shalt not'. God knows the sinfulness of the human mind. A command to not do something is, to erring humans, almost an invitation to do the opposite. Consider the itch you get when you see the sign saying, 'wet paint – don't touch'; your hand twitches to touch it, to see if it is still wet. God designed the law to emphasise our sinfulness. Paul puts it this way: *"that*

---

[3]Luke 24.27

[4]Luke 24.44-45

sin by the commandment might become exceeding sinful"[5]. The Ten Commandments were written to highlight the serious nature of the offence. Paul says, "*the law entered, that the offence might abound*"[6] and "*sin might appear sin*"[7]. They were also written to warn of impending judgment if broken: "*the law worketh wrath.*"[8]

James warns that we cannot choose which commands we intend to obey; the Ten Commandments hang together as whole. If we break one, we have broken them all[9].

3. The Law emphasises our need of the Saviour

The Ten Commandments and the wider books of law could not save. They could only expose sin and show the need of a Saviour. The Hebrew writer says, "*the law made nothing perfect*"[10] but then adds, speaking of the coming into the world of the Lord Jesus Christ, "*the bringing in of a better hope did.*" Those who seek to work hard for salvation have missed the whole point of the law. We cannot be saved by good works[11]; the law shows that we have sinned and need forgiveness. Even what we regard as our best works are *filthy rags* in God's sight.[12]

---

[5]Romans 7.13

[6]Romans 5.20

[7]Romans 7.13

[8]Romans 4.15

[9]James 2.10: "For whosoever shall keep the whole law, and yet offend in one *point*, he is guilty of all."

[10]Hebrews 7.19

[11]Ephesians 2.8-9: "For by grace are ye saved through faith; and that not of yourselves: it is the gift of God: Not of works, lest any man should boast."

[12]Isaiah 64.6: "But we are all as an unclean thing, and all our righteousnesses are as filthy rags; and we all do fade as a leaf; and our iniquities, like the wind, have taken us away."

The rich young ruler thought that he could do something to inherit eternal life: indeed, he thought he could do good works.[13] The Lord Jesus tested his understanding of the word 'good', the character of God and the identity of Himself as God, telling him that there *"was none good but one, that is, God"*[14]. He also tested him on his keeping of the law. The rich ruler thought he had kept all the Ten Commandments which showed how little he understood of the character of God, the purpose of the law and, indeed, the sin of his own heart. The Lord tested him on commandment number 10 ('Thou shalt not covet') and he failed; he loved material things. Sadly, we never read of that man coming to realise that the law had brought him to Christ for salvation. He went "away sorrowful" still apparently trusting, like so many others, in the keeping of the law to inherit eternal life. How very sad!

The purpose of the law, however, was to bring us to see the need of Christ. Paul puts it this way: *"Wherefore the law was our schoolmaster ('pedagogue') to bring us unto Christ, that we might be justified by faith. But after that faith is come, we are no longer under a schoolmaster"*[15].

Once we have taken Christ as Saviour, we graduate from the school of law to that of grace. Paul says *"ye are not under the law, but under grace."*[16] We are justified (constituted righteous) by faith in Christ and now we no longer fear the judgment of God for our sin because we understand that Christ has died for our sins. In the Epistle to the Romans the metaphor of marriage is used to describe the transition from law to Christ: *"Wherefore, my brethren,*

---

[13]Matthew 19.16: "Good Master, what good thing shall I do, that I may have eternal life?"

[14]Matthew 19.17

[15]Galatians 3.24-25

[16]Romans 6.14

ye also are become dead to the law by the body of Christ; that ye should be married to another, even to him who is raised from the dead, that we should bring forth fruit unto God"[17]. The fearsome judgments of the law that condemned us have been taken away in the death and resurrection of Christ. Paul says: *"having forgiven you all trespasses; Blotting out the handwriting of ordinances that was against us, which was contrary to us, and took it out of the way, nailing it to his cross"*[18]. *"Christ is the end of the law for righteousness"*[19]. This means that the work of Christ on Calvary ends the possibility of the law being a means to attaining righteousness. Instead, each believer in Christ is given, as a free gift, the righteousness of God on the basis of grace by faith[20]. Hallelujah, what a Saviour!

As Christians we are no longer under the law[21] and should never desire to be so again.[22] However, this does not mean that the law is now unspiritual and not required; far from it. Paul says the *"law is holy, and the commandment holy, and just, and good"*[23]. However, it does mean that we need to understand the purpose of the law. It cannot convert but it can convict.

---

[17]Romans 7.4

[18]Colossians 2.13-14

[19]Romans 10.4

[20]Romans 4.25 - 5.1: "Who was delivered for our offences, and was raised again for our justification. Therefore being justified by faith, we have peace with God through our Lord Jesus Christ".

[21]Romans 6.14 "For sin shall not have dominion over you: for ye are not under the law, but under grace".

[22]Galatians 4.21 "Tell me, ye that desire to be under the law, do ye not hear the law?"

[23]Romans 7.12

4. The Law is to be fulfilled in the life of believers

The law was designed to bring blessing if obeyed. Moses said to Israel on the plains of Moab that it was for their good: "*Keep the commandments of the LORD, and his statutes, which I command thee this day for thy good*" (Deuteronomy 10.13). Moses speaks of positive blessings that come from obedience to the law in Leviticus chapter 26.1-13 and then further warns throughout the remainder of the chapter that disobeying the commandments[24] will impact on their health, environment and life. It was the Saviour who spoke of life to be found in keeping the commandments: "*if thou wilt enter into life, keep the commandments*"[25]. Israel, sadly, never discovered the blessings of the law. The believer today, however, can fulfil the law and enter its blessings[26].

Believers in the Lord Jesus have received the Holy Spirit[27]. Their bodies are now "*the temple of the Holy Spirit*"[28]. We now have a new power to live for God and bring forth fruit to God. What

---

[24]Lev 26.14-16: "But if ye will not hearken unto me, and will not do all these commandments; And if ye shall despise my statutes, or if your soul abhor my judgments, so that ye will not do all my commandments, but that ye break my covenant: I also will do this unto you; I will even appoint over you terror, consumption, and the burning ague, that shall consume the eyes, and cause sorrow of heart: and ye shall sow your seed in vain, for your enemies shall eat it."

[25]Matthew 19.17

[26]Romans 13.8: "Owe no man any thing, but to love one another: for he that loveth another hath fulfilled the law."

[27]Ephesians 1.13: "in whom also after that ye believed *(Literally: upon believing)*, ye were sealed with that Holy Spirit of promise."

[28]1 Corinthians 6.19

condemned me before salvation[29] can now be liberating truth[30]. We can be slaves to righteousness instead of slaves to sin. Paul states so beautifully: *"That the righteousness of the law might be fulfilled in us, who walk not after the flesh, but after the Spirit"*[31]. Therefore, Christians cannot say that the Ten Commandments do not apply today. We can, however, only fulfil the righteousness of the law by the power of the Holy Spirit. In our own strength, we will fail every time.

When we were unsaved we were under the law and had no real capacity to please God. But once we were saved and we received the Holy Spirit[32] indwelling us, we are no longer under law's bondage and claims.[33] We are now motivated by a new principle - Christ. We are now *"under law to Christ"*[34]. It is His words and commands that motivate us and it is through His power that we can fulfil 'the righteousness of the law of God'.

---

[29]Romans 6.20-21: "For when ye were the servants of sin (i.e. *before salvation*), ye were free from righteousness. What fruit had ye then (i.e. before salvation) in those things whereof ye are now ashamed? for the end of those things is death."

[30]Romans 6.17-18: "But God be thanked, that ye were the servants of sin, but ye have obeyed from the heart that form of doctrine which was delivered you. Being then made free from sin, ye became the servants of righteousness."

[31]Romans 8.4

[32]Ephesians 1.13: "In whom also after that ye believed, ye were sealed with that holy Spirit of promise."

[33]Galatians 5.18: "But if ye be led of the Spirit, ye are not under the law."

[34]1 Corinthians 9.12

The Lord's ministry on the Ten Commandments in what is often called the Sermon on the Mount (Matthew 5-7) is critical. He expands upon the principles that should govern our minds and behaviour, as God's people. He said, that upon His interpretation of the Ten Commandments *'hang all the law and the prophets'*[35]. Therefore they are essential for the believer today.

This world itself is lacking even a semblance of these divine principles in daily life and is reaping the consequences of a materialistic, selfish lifestyle. Let us, as Christians, live by the principles of God's commandments.

Therefore, when we read and meditate on the Ten Commandments we need to consider their fourfold purpose to:

• Reveal the supreme glory of Christ
• Expose sin and judgment in our life
• Emphasise our need of the Saviour
• Fulfil God's will in our life so that we live in harmony with God and each other.

Therefore, we must ensure that we understand what 'the law' means for us today taking into account the full revelation of the Word of God.

---

[35]Matthew 22.36-40

Notes

_____

_____

_____

_____

_____

_____

_____

_____

_____

_____

_____

Commandment 1

Thou Shalt Have No Other Gods Before Me

"I am the LORD thy God, which have brought thee out of the land of Egypt, out of the house of bondage. Thou shalt have no other gods before (beside) me."

Exodus 20.2-3

Attribute: Solitariness of God
Principle: Response to the Uniqueness of God

God is unique. He is a solitary God. He cannot be compared with anything or anyone else. In the beginning there was God, and God alone. There was no sun, no stars, no heaven, no earth, no angels or men, no universe, nothing, no one, but God.

God was alone not merely for a week, a year, or an age, but from *everlasting*[36]. God needed nothing[37]. When He created a universe or angels or men it added nothing to God essentially. He *"changes not."*[38] His essential glory can neither be enhanced nor diminished.

---

[36]Psalm 90.2: "from everlasting to everlasting, thou art God."

[37]Acts 17.25: "Neither is worshipped with men's hands, as though he needed anything, seeing he giveth to all life, and breath, and all things."

[38]Malachi 3.6: "For I *am* the LORD, I change not; therefore ye sons of Jacob are not consumed."

God was under no constraint to create: when He did create it was simply for His glory; for He *"worketh all things after the counsel of his own will."*[39] The creation concludes that there must be a Creator; the design demonstrates a Designer. The human race is *"without excuse"*[40] as the evidence of the glory of God is overwhelming. Yet Job maintained that the vast universe was merely a *"little whisper"* of the revelation of His glory[41]. What is astonishing is that He should reveal anything of His unique glory to human beings at all.

Yet, in this first commandment God does not justify His unique right as being the only God on the grounds of Him being our Creator. His right to claim the unique position as God is because He is the Redeemer God: *"I am the LORD thy God, which brought thee out of the land of Egypt, out of the house of bondage"*[42]. The Ten Commandments commence with a reminder of the love of a redeeming God. God is love[43], and uniquely so. He is a redeemer God – a God who purchased His people with the blood of the Passover lamb (Exodus 12) and delivered His people in mighty power at the Red Sea (Exodus 14-15). Israel would not have needed any reminder of His redemption at the Red Sea. When God had redeemed them, they sang by the seashore of His

---

[39]Ephesians 1.11

[40]Romans 1.20: "For the invisible things of him from the creation of the world are clearly seen, being understood by the things that are made, *even* his eternal power and Godhead; so that they are without excuse."

[41]Job 26.14: "Lo, these *are* parts of his ways: but how little a portion (margin: little whisper) is heard of him?"

[42]Exodus 20.2

[43]1 John 4.8: "He that loveth not knoweth not God; for God is love."

uniqueness: *"Who is like unto thee, O LORD, among the gods? Who is like thee, glorious in holiness, fearful in praises, doing wonders?"*[44].

Yet, sadly, it was only a short time before those who were redeemed through the Red Sea would forget the unique glory of God and turn to other things, including false gods. What about God's people today? Are we not just as fickle as Israel of old? Would we have needed any reminder of the uniqueness of God on our conversion day? We also have been purchased. God has asserted His right in grace to own us through the payment of the ransom price of the blood of Christ for all[45]. He legally owns us: *"For ye are bought with a price: therefore glorify God in your body, and in your spirit, which are God's"*[46].

Has Christ not delivered us also from the bondage of sin? Has He not placed sea between Egypt (a picture of the world) and every believer? The Scriptures teach us that Christ: *"gave himself for our sins that he might deliver us from this present evil world"*[47]. We have been delivered from the world's claim upon us and should now live lives that are different to its attitudes and methods and we must stay separated from its systems. Paul warns that the cross of Calvary separates us from the world and that we should see the world in all its various facets, for example, religion, fashions, sport, music etc. for what it is, through the lens of the cross[48]. John

---

[44]Exodus 15.11

[45]1 Timothy 2.6: "Who gave himself a ransom for all, to be testified in due time."

[46]1 Corinthians 6.20

[47]Galatians 1.4

[48]Galatians 6.14: "But God forbid that I should glory, save in the cross of our Lord Jesus Christ, by whom the world is crucified unto me, and I unto the world."

is equally as blunt about the Christian's position to the world[49]. He says those that love the world are not saved.

Israel had some appreciation that redemption brought future blessing as they also sang at the Red Sea that God would *"bring them in to the place, O LORD, which thou hast made for thee to dwell in in the Sanctuary, O Lord"*[50].

Perhaps we also have forgotten that a unique feature of Calvary is not only to deliver us from the gods of this world and from self but also to display something of the unique glories of Christ in our lives and bring us into the glory of His Sanctuary, His House. He has redeemed us to Himself. Believers have been not only *"brought out"* of the world but they can be *"brought in"* to the "place" where He "dwells"[51] on earth – the House of God. The early Christians gathered together to the Name of the Lord Jesus after they had been gathered out of the world[52].

---

[49]1 John 2.15: "Love not the world, neither the things that are in the world. If any man love the world, the love of the Father is not in him."

[50]Exodus 15.17: "Thou shalt bring them in, and plant them in the mountain of thine inheritance, *in* the place, O LORD, *which* thou hast made for thee to dwell in, *in* the Sanctuary, O Lord, *which* thy hands have established."

[51]Deuteronomy 6.23: "And he brought us out from thence, that he might bring us in";

Deuteronomy 12.14 "But in the place which the LORD shall choose in one of thy tribes, there thou shalt offer";

Matt. 18.20: "For where two or three are gathered together in my name, there am I in the midst of them."

[52]Hebrews 13.13-14; Acts 2.41-42; 1 Tim. 3.15; 1 Cor. 5.4,12; 11.18, 20.

God is a unique God and has no rivals. And yet, the Triune God has amazingly chosen to be revealed. This full and final revelation is only through His Son, the Lord Jesus. He is the unique revealer of the solitary God: *"No man hath seen God at any time; the only begotten Son, which is in the bosom of the Father, he hath declared him"*[53].

The Lord Jesus Christ declared the power of God over death, disease, and the devil. He declared the righteousness of God in His pure and sinless life and in His death "for sins[54]." He declared the care and kindness of God in His interest and sympathy for people in difficulty and despair. He displayed the love of God in His death for a rebellious world. We saw the tear trickle down His lovely face near the grave of Lazarus. We heard Him wail over Jerusalem. He spoke the words of God – every word was inspired, Holy Spirit breathed. He did the works of God and the will of God. His motive, His manner and His methods were all a revelation of the greatness of God. None can be compared to the Lord Jesus. It is *"in Him"* that we have "*redemption*"[55] and it is "*for Him*" and "*to Him*" that we have been saved[56].

---

[53]John 1.18

[54]Romans 3.25-26: "Whom God hath set forth to be a propitiation through faith in his blood, to declare his righteousness for the remission of sins that are past, through the forbearance of God; To declare, I say, at this time his righteousness: that he might be just, and the justifier of him which believeth in Jesus";

Hebrews 10.12: "But this man, after he had offered one sacrifice for sins for ever, sat down on the right hand of God."

[55]Ephesians 1.7

[56]Romans 11.36

Have we lost sight of His glory? Have "other gods" excluded His glory from our hearts? Perhaps the cares of this world have dampened enthusiasm for Him. Possibly the pleasures of this world are consuming our time and passions to the exclusion of Him. Where do our affections lie? Can we say with Paul: *"For to me to live is Christ"*[57]? Is it not humbling to realise that the "solitary" God is still interested in us.

An appreciation of the uniqueness of our "redeemer God" will result in us loving Him with all our heart and soul and mind[58]. Love for Him will take precedence over relatives and friends[59] and will result in reproach and if necessary will require the loss of all things for Him[60].

In the light of all of this, perhaps we all need to hear again the first commandment from the heart of God, *"I am the LORD thy God, which have brought thee out of the land of Egypt, out of the house of bondage. Thou shalt have no other gods before (beside) me."*

---

[57]Philippians 1.21

[58]Matthew 22.37

[59]Luke 14.26: "If any man come to me, and hate not his father, and mother, and wife, and children, and brethren, and sisters, yea, and his own life also, he cannot be my disciple."

[60]Luke 14.33: "whosoever he be of you that forsaketh not all that he hath, he cannot be my disciple."

Notes

Notes

Commandment 2

Thou Shalt Not Make Unto Thee Any Graven Image

"Thou shalt not make unto thee any graven image, or any likeness of any thing that is in heaven above, or that is in the earth beneath, or that is in the water under the earth: Thou shalt not bow down thyself to them, nor serve them: for I the LORD thy God am a jealous God, visiting the iniquity of the fathers upon the children unto the third and fourth generation of them that hate me; And showing mercy unto thousands of them that love me, and keep my commandments."

Exodus 20. 3-6

Attribute: Supremacy of God
Principle: Recognition of the Jealousy of God

God is incomprehensible. The human mind is incapable of fully comprehending Him; human language is inadequate when describing Him; time is too limited to declare Him; human creativity is too superficial to display Him.

The Lord knew the human tendency to simplify matters and desire to appear to have mastery over everything. He was so careful over the glimpse of His glory that He revealed on Sinai. He said, *"you saw no manner of similitude on the day that the LORD spake unto you in Horeb out of the midst of the fire: lest ye corrupt yourselves and make you a graven image."*[61] No image or resemblance made by human hands can have any link with His glory. God is supreme.

Over earth's varying chronologies and geographies humans have made images of gold, silver, wood, and stone and venerated them as God. But God hates this idolatry and condemns it in this second commandment. Lest anyone should think that this primitive idea is irrelevant in the 21st century, it is worth remembering that due to the population of earth continuing to increase there are more idols of gold today than at any period of human history.

The Scripture records the connection between the creator of idols and the idols themselves: *"they that make them are like unto them."*[62] In other words, the idols are made in the image of man – in contradistinction to *"man being made in the image of God."*[63] This principle of idolatry pervades every culture. Humans are placed first.

Man-made thoughts about God often result in false teaching about God. It may well have been the case that the Israelites did not think the golden calf was God (particularly as it was only forty days after the second commandment was uttered); but they did think that in some way it resembled God. Perhaps they had thoughts about it being a clean animal, made of gold etc.

---

[61]Deuteronomy 4.15

[62]Psalm 135.18

[63]Genesis 1.26-27

However, this led onto the claim: *"These be thy gods, O Israel"*[64] and the subsequent revelry. The consequences of their actions revealed the gravity of their error. Moses broke the calf in pieces, ground it to powder, and then forced the people of God to drink of the dust as a powerful indication of the dreadfulness of their sin[65]. We must be very careful what we think and say about the incomprehensible God.

The incomprehensible God has only one image - that is His Son, the Lord Jesus. He is *"the image of the invisible God"*[66]. He is *"the effulgence of his glory, the expression of his substance"*[67]. When God became a man in the person of His Son then a full declaration of His glory was fully represented in Him[68]. Humans could touch, feel, and hear Him. He said: *"He that hath seen me hath seen the Father."*[69] We can listen to His words, watch His actions and reactions, and learn daily something of the character of the incomprehensible God. What a privilege believers have to meditate upon the person of Christ and learn something of the heart of God. But, of course, we can only do this through the power of the Holy Spirit. Human reasoning will never explain, for example, the Trinity, the virgin birth, the expiatory sacrifice at Calvary. The Christ of God is truly incomprehensible.

---

[64]Exodus 32. 4

[65]Exodus 32.20

[66]Colossians 1.15

[67]Hebrews 1.2-3 (Darby)

[68]John 1.18: "No man hath seen God at any time; the only begotten Son, which is in the bosom of the Father, he hath declared *him*".

[69]John 14. 9

What will happen if we serve another? What will happen if we apply human thinking to the incomprehensible Christ? We will learn then that God is a *"jealous God."* This is a title used seven times in Scripture[70] and a further nineteen times in the Bible God is described as jealous.

We can be sure that His jealousy is not sinful. The motivating principle for His anger is that He is jealous for our obedience. His glory demands this as Creator and Redeemer. His jealous anger will be directed against all idolaters and those who have false thoughts about Him. This commandment is not suggesting that if one person sins then his or her children will be judged as well. This was the false idea the people of Ezekiel's day had on this verse, saying: *"The fathers have eaten sour grapes, and the children's teeth are set on edge"*[71]. This human proverb meant that because of the sin of the fathers, the children could expect judgment. Ezekiel had to explain that this is not true. *"The son shall not bear the iniquity of the father, neither shall the father bear the iniquity of the son."*[72] Everyone is responsible to God for their own life and will never be held accountable for the sins of their parents.

However, the second command about judgment on future generations is still true. God deals with nations in this way, including Israel during the Exile. Where rank idolatry is to be found then God often judges that nation for several generations until they learn *"that the Most High rules in the kingdom of men"*[73]. We should remember the solemn fact that our sin can often stumble

---

[70]Ex. 20.5; 34.14; Deut. 4.24; 5:9; 6.15; Josh. 24.19; Nahum 1.2

[71]Ezekiel 18.2

[72]Ezekiel 18.20

[73]Daniel 4.17

subsequent generations. The corollary is also true: where honour and reverence to Him are found then mercy and love is requited; *"showing mercy unto thousands of them that love me."* Jehovah desires our affection and desires that we all honour His supremacy.

What about believers today? Are we in the good of this second commandment? Is our heart hot for Him? Let us be on our guard. Carnality and love of the world's idols have caused God's people to fall from generation to generation. Do we need to hear the words of John again *"Little children, keep yourselves from idols"*[74]? Paul warns that Christians should not be found in idol's temples, likening it to fellowship with demons[75]. Is there not a need for collective repentance amongst God's people and a separating from all that is evil? Are *"we provoking the Lord to jealousy?"*[76] Listen again to the second commandment, *"Thou shalt **not make unto thee any graven image**, or any likeness of any thing that is in heaven above, or that is in the earth beneath, or that is in the water under the earth: Thou shalt not bow down thyself to them, nor serve them: for I the LORD thy God am a **jealous God**, visiting the iniquity of the fathers upon the children unto the third and fourth generation of them that hate me; And **showing mercy** unto thousands of them that love me, and keep my commandments" (Exodus 20.3-6).*

---

[74] 1 John 5. 21

[75] 1 Cor. 10.20-21: "But I say, that the things which the Gentiles sacrifice, they sacrifice to devils, and not to God: and I would not that ye should have fellowship with devils. Ye cannot drink the cup of the Lord, and the cup of devils: ye cannot be partakers of the Lord's table, and of the table of devils."

[76] 1 Cor. 10.22

Notes

Notes

Commandment 3

Thou Shalt Not Take The Name Of The Lord Thy God In Vain

"Thou shalt not take the name of the LORD thy God in vain; for the LORD will not hold him guiltless that taketh his name in vain."

Exodus 20.7

Attribute: Sovereignty of God
Principle: Reverence for the Name of God

God's Name is to be revered. God's name speaks of His character. It encompasses all His divine attributes. He is unique, sovereign, and incomprehensible. We should be careful in our approach to Him, and as we speak about Him. There should be nothing familiar in our language as we address God.

In the first place, the name of God should be used with reverence. Profane language is an insult to God and should never be on the lips of a believer. We should not become accustomed to the world's curses and insults remembering that it is His enemies that take His name in vain[77]. Loose language about God is not acceptable and the Christian should stand out by the way they speak to God and of God.

Second, we also should never use the name of God to affirm truth – we should be men and woman of our word[78]. Oaths and swearing of allegiance in His name is strictly forbidden. In a dishonest world let our yes mean yes and our no mean no[79].

Third, doubting the faithfulness of God or a lack of dependence upon Him is taking the Name of the Lord in vain. Agur could say, *"Give me neither poverty nor riches .... lest I be full, and deny thee, and say, Who is the LORD? or lest I be poor, and steal, and take the name of my God in vain"*[80]. Agur was conscious that human weakness could result in taking the name of the Lord in vain. Riches may lead him to question his dependency upon God; poverty may lead him to question the faithfulness of God. Have you ever experienced this?

---

[77]Lev. 24:13-16: "...And thou shalt speak unto the children of Israel, saying, whosoever curseth his God shall bear his sin. And he that blasphemeth the name of the LORD, he shall surely be put to death..."; Ps.139:20: "For they speak against thee wickedly, *and* thine enemies take *thy name* in vain."

[78]Matthew 5.34-37: "But I say unto you, Swear not at all; neither by heaven; for it is God's throne: Nor by the earth; for it is his footstool: neither by Jerusalem; for it is the city of the great King. Neither shalt thou swear by thy head, because thou canst not make one hair white or black. But let your communication be, Yea, yea; Nay, nay: for whatsoever is more than these cometh of evil."

[79]2 Cor. 1.17-19: "...When I therefore was thus minded, did I use lightness? or the things that I purpose, do I purpose according to the flesh, that with me there should be yea yea, and nay nay? But as God is true, our word toward you was not yea and nay. For the Son of God, Jesus Christ, who was preached among you by us, even by me and Silvanus and Timotheus, was not yea and nay, but in him was yea. For all the promises of God in him are yea, and in him Amen, unto the glory of God by us."

[80]Proverbs 30.8-9

Perhaps unuttered thoughts have arisen in our heart making us question something of the character of God. We should shudder at the first stirring of unbelief! This was a wise prayer of Agur, for the Lord would not hold him guiltless.

A fourth way to take the name of the Lord our God in vain is to associate His name with something false. Ten of the tribes worshipped the calf at Bethel but it was an affront to the character of God and something that was ultimately judged by God[81]. The old prophet who misled the man of God[82] by claiming that the Lord had spoken to him is an example of a man who implicated the Lord in a message that really originated in his own mind, not God's. He reaped the consequences. Is there a reader who is knowingly pursuing a work for the "Lord" in a manner that he/she knows to be unscriptural? This is taking the name of the Lord in vain.

A fifth way to take the name of the Lord in vain is to imbibe false superstitious notions. Jeremiah said, *"Truly in vain is salvation hoped for from the hills, ... truly in the LORD our God is the salvation of Israel"*[83]. Clearly there were those who thought the hills could save them! This called into question the Lord's strength to save! Amongst the Lord's people false notions or superstitions sometimes become apparent. If we examined these carefully it would surprise us how pagan their origins are. Let us cleanse ourselves from anything that calls us to question the character of God or causes us to depend on anything else but Him. *"And they that know thy name will put their trust in thee"*[84].

---

[81]Amos 4.4; 5.5; 7.1-17; 9.1-5

[82]1 Kings 13:11-34

[83]Jeremiah 3.23

[84]Psalm 9.10

Sixth, through religious legalism we can take the name of the Lord our God in vain. The Lord said of the Pharisees, *"But in vain they do worship me, teaching for doctrines the commandments of men"*[85]. Their commandments appeared to be very holy and spiritual but they contradicted and added to the Word of God. Anything that replaces the clear Word of God is an insult to the authority of God. Legalism often lurks in the most liberal of places. Anything that forces through a form of worship or man-made liturgy as the divine standard, or rules of conscience as doctrine, or vigorously presents dogmas which are based upon an unbalanced theology, is taking the name of the Lord in vain. How careful we ought to be!

Finally, and seventh, is there a perfect interpretation of the Name of the Lord? The simple answer is, yes. *"For unto us a child is born, unto us a son is given: and the government shall be upon his shoulder: and his name shall be called Wonderful, Counsellor, The mighty God, The everlasting Father, The Prince of Peace"*[86].

The Lord Jesus is the "Word"[87], the full expression of God. The character of God is fully represented and declared in Him[88]. Israel will never know deliverance until they heed His words, *"Ye shall not see me henceforth, till ye shall say, Blessed [is] he that cometh in the name of the Lord."*[89] Let us be careful how we think and speak of Him. Let us never forget the third commandment: *"**Thou shalt not take the name of the LORD thy God in vain; for the LORD will not hold him guiltless that taketh his name in vain.**"*

---

[85]Matthew 15.9

[86]Isaiah 9.6

[87]John 1.1

[88]John 1.18: "No man hath seen God at any time; the only begotten Son, which is in the bosom of the Father, he hath declared him."

[89]Matthew 23.39

Notes

Notes

Commandment 4

Remember The Sabbath Day To Keep It Holy

"Remember the sabbath day, to keep it holy. Six days shalt thou labour, and do all thy work: But the seventh day is the sabbath of the LORD thy God: in it thou shalt not do any work, thou, nor thy son, nor thy daughter."

Exodus 20.8-11

Attribute: Sanctity of God
Principle: Respect for the Rest of God

God is wise. He set aside a day uniquely for Himself. It was the day that He rested after completing the work of creation. This does not mean that God did nothing at all on the seventh day. The enormous work of *sustaining*[90] the stellar heavens and being guardian and governor of the universe, continually giving life and breath to the world[91] all took place on the seventh day. The Lord Jesus spoke of His Father's work on the seventh day[92]. New acts

---

[90]Heb. 1.3: "and upholding (*word means an active preservation not a static custodian*) all things by the word of his power."

[91]Acts 17.25: "seeing he giveth to all life, and breath, and all things."

[92]John 5.16-17: "And therefore did the Jews persecute Jesus, and sought to slay him, because he had done these things on the sabbath day. But Jesus answered them, My Father worketh hitherto, and I work."

of creation were, however, not accomplished on the seventh day. This principle of enjoying rest was brought before the people in Exodus 16 for the first time[93]. On Mount Sinai, it is stated again directly, and strangers and animals are included. It was a binding law upon the people that would bring death if broken[94]. A sabbatical every seventh year was also binding upon the land[95]. Failure to keep the agricultural Sabbaths would result in God's judgment[96].

However, the Lord did not teach that we should keep the Sabbath in His unfolding of the commandments in Matthew chapters 5-7. Many of His miracles were performed on this day as He highlighted the hypocrisy of the Pharisees' making rules for the Sabbath. Paul specifically says that today we should not keep any day special, neither the Sabbath day, nor any other Jewish festival day[97] and warned seriously against those who tried to enforce this on others. He condemned the Galatians for the same error:

---

[93]Exodus 16.23: "Tomorrow is the rest of the holy sabbath unto the LORD."

[94]Exodus 31.14-15: "Ye shall keep the sabbath therefore; for it is holy unto you: everyone that defileth it shall surely be put to death: for whosoever doeth any work therein, that soul shall be cut off from among his people. Six days may work be done; but in the seventh is the sabbath of rest, holy to the LORD: whosoever doeth any work in the sabbath day, he shall surely be put to death"; (C.f. Numbers 15.32-36)

[95]Leviticus 25.4: "But in the seventh year shall be a sabbath of rest unto the land, a sabbath for the LORD: thou shalt neither sow thy field, nor prune thy vineyard."

[96]2 Chronicles 36.21: "To fulfil the word of the LORD by the mouth of Jeremiah, until the land had enjoyed her sabbaths: for as long as she lay desolate she kept sabbath, to fulfil threescore and ten years."

[97]Col. 2.16-17: "Let no man therefore judge you in meat, or in drink, or in respect of an holyday, or of the new moon, or of the sabbath days: Which are a shadow of things to come; but the body (substance) is of Christ."

"Ye observe days, and months, and times, and years"[98]. His teaching is clear that we are no longer under law[99] and we have no desire to go back and be under its bondage[100]. The Christian is not asked to literally observe Saturday as special and those who insist on this, are condemned by the Apostle Paul as false teachers.

Does this mean, therefore, that this commandment is irrelevant today? Far from it! In the strongest terms, we refute this. This commandment is God's Word and essential for us today.

First, there is the simple fact God created weeks for the benefit of human beings. The Sabbath was the end of the week and in it there was to be rest. The principle of a rest every seven days is a good one. Despite no meteorological or astrological reason for weeks (unlike days, months, and years) all civilizations across our globe still operate in weeks. This is an incredible evidence for God's creation. In our 'dot-com' culture of instant communications and services open 24/7 the need for rest once a week is still as essential and valid as it was on the day it was created.

This rest includes physical rest. It was the Saviour who said,

---

[98]Galatians 4.10 – it is interesting that Paul omits 'weeks' here. The only time we are asked to keep – Acts 20.7.

[99]Romans 7.4: "Wherefore, my brethren, ye also are become dead to the law by the body of Christ; that ye should be married to another, even to him who is raised from the dead, that we should bring forth fruit unto God."

[100]Galatians 4.9, 11: "But now, after that ye have known God, or rather are known of God, how turn ye again to the weak and beggarly elements, whereunto ye desire again to be in bondage? ... I am afraid of you, lest I have bestowed upon you labour in vain."

"*Sleep on now and take your rest*"[101] and Scripture warns of staying up too late "*for so he giveth his beloved sleep*"[102]. It was food and rest that a depressed Elijah needed more than anything else when he ran away from Jezebel[103].

We also need to take time out for the things that matter. We are all affected by the pursuit of material things all around us. For example, many couples are working all hours of the day to pay the mortgage and maintain the lifestyle that they seek, but may be missing the rest and peace that God would want them to enjoy. We are very painfully aware that some saints are in situations that they did not choose and could not foresee and there is no criticism intended at all here. Sadly, however, it is also true that many are sacrificing on the altar of activity their marriage, their family, the assembly, and their relationship with God. In some cases, we may have to take a cut in salary and work fewer hours to save our marriage, our families, our enjoyment of the Lord and the assembly of God's people.

Intensive farming and manufacturing methods and the desire to make money every second of the day has resulted in working practices far removed from God's original intentions. The land

---

[101]Matthew 26.45

[102]Psalm 127.2

[103]"1 Kings 19.5-8: "And as he lay and slept under a juniper tree, behold, then an angel touched him, and said unto him, Arise and eat. And he looked, and, behold, there was a cake baken on the coals, and a cruse of water at his head. And he did eat and drink, and laid him down again. And the angel of the LORD came again the second time, and touched him, and said, Arise and eat; because the journey is too great for thee. And he arose, and did eat and drink, and went in the strength of that meat forty days and forty nights unto Horeb the mount of God."

and sea need to rest as well and if we do not obey this instruction we shall soon find that fish stocks and crop yields will be depleted. Automation, artificial stimulants, and genetically modified foods can temporarily extend productivity and drive down prices for food but they are no substitute for the world of creation being at rest with mankind.

Second, the spiritual meaning of the Sabbath as outlined in the New Testament is the principle of "rest". This is the basis of the "salvation" that we enjoy in Christ. Behind the "rest" of creation was the greater "rest" of redemption. We learn in Hebrews that we must *cease from our works*[104] and *"through faith"* rest upon Christ. Our salvation is by grace through faith in Christ *"and not of works lest any man should boast."*[105] There is a Sabbath rest in Him for the people of God[106]. Anxiety and trouble are all around us, but the Christian has settled peace with God[107].

After the 'rest' of salvation, as we make spiritual progress, we can enjoy the rest of fellowship and obedience. If we compare the two "rests" in Matthew 11.28-29[108] we will learn there is the rest of **salvation** that is a gift from Christ (*'Come unto me and I will give*

---

[104]Hebrews 4.10: "For he that is entered into his rest, he also hath ceased from his own works, as God *did* from his."

[105]Ephesians 2.8: "For by grace are ye saved through faith; and that not of yourselves: it is the gift of God: Not of works, lest any man should boast."

[106]Hebrews 4.9: "There remaineth therefore a [Sabbath] rest to the people of God."

[107]Romans 5.1: "Therefore being justified by faith, we have peace with God through our Lord Jesus Christ."

[108]Matthew 11.28-29: "Come unto me, all ye that labour and are heavy laden, and I will give you rest. Take my yoke upon you, and learn of me; for I am meek and lowly in heart: and ye shall find rest unto your souls."

you rest') and then there is rest of **communion** as we progress spiritually entering and enjoy fellowship with Christ (*'Learn of me and ye shall find rest'*). There is also a further thought of rest in God's House[109] as we learn to be baptised and join a fellowship of God's people who gather to the Name of the Lord Jesus alone and come to the House *"of My rest"*. Are we enjoying this rest? It is good to rest and enjoy what God is resting in. Rest will then become a feature of the believer just like Solomon who was called "a man of rest'. We do, as Christians, need to actively engage in resting in the Lord. That is why the Psalmist had to say: *"Rest in the LORD, and wait patiently for him* (Psalm 37.7)"; *"For David said, The LORD God of Israel hath given rest unto his people, that they may dwell in Jerusalem forever* (1 Chronicles 23.25)"; *"Behold, a son shall be born to thee, who shall be a man of rest; and I will give him rest from all his enemies round about: for his name shall be Solomon, and I will give peace and quietness unto Israel in his days"* (1 Chronicles 22.9)."

Third, there is a practical lesson for us regarding how busy we are. The Sabbath for Israel was set in contrast to the seven days a week labour to Pharaoh in Egypt. *"And remember that thou wast a servant in the land of Egypt… therefore the LORD thy God commanded thee to keep the sabbath day"*[110]. We also live busy lives and the world will see to it that we are consumed seven days a week, so that we never enjoy the "rest" of Christ. There is a need to *"come ye yourselves apart and rest a while."*[111] The first day of the week is a special day for the Christian. It was the day that time was

---

[109]Acts 7.49: "Heaven *is* my throne, and earth *is* my footstool: what house will ye build me? saith the Lord: or what *is* the place of my rest?";
Psalm 132.7-8: "We will go into his tabernacles: we will worship at his footstool. Arise, O LORD, into thy rest; thou, and the ark of thy strength."

[110]Deuteronomy 5.15

[111]Mark 6.31

created[112], the day the Lord Jesus rose again from the dead, it was the day of Pentecost when the church was created (Acts 2), the day when disciples broke bread[113] in the weekly remembrance of Christ. Without rule making, let us make sure that whenever possible we are enjoying the "rest" of Christ on that day and not taken up with the everyday, even legitimate, objectives. God knows what is good for us.

Different cultures and societies sometimes do not allow the first day of the week to be set aside for Him entirely and demand secular work on that day. This was the case in the time of the apostles. The Lord knows and understands and will guide His people in these circumstances. Thankfully, this is not the case for many of us. Whilst we fully accept that some vocations and professions, such as those working in the medical professions, must be available on every day of the week, as Christians we still need to think very carefully about the career we go in for, to be free for the gatherings of the Lord's people on the Lord's day as much as possible. Irrespective of our circumstances, the first collective exercise for the week should always be the Breaking of Bread. The principle in Scripture is 'God first': worship before service. Interestingly, the priests were busier on the Sabbath day than any other day of the week - more flour, more bread, more

---

[112]Gen. 1.1

[113]Acts 20.7: "And upon the first day of the week, when the disciples came together to break bread." It does not say 'the disciples came together' but 'when the disciples came together' – this was their practice to come together on this day to break bread. It does not say that they came together to hear Paul preach. They would have come together anyway - it was their practice to break bread on this day. After the breaking of bread Paul took the opportunity to preach.

lambs on that day than any other day[114]. It is appropriate for saints to be busier in spiritual things on the first day of the week than any other day. We should, however, be careful not to exhaust God's people! Furthermore, we do not serve the Lord only on a Sunday. Every day is for the Lord.

Fourth, the Sabbath makes us think of Christ. He is the *"Lord of the Sabbath"*[115]. The Lord Jesus walked in the fields, made men see, made a woman straight, and gave a man the power of his hand, all on the Sabbath day. He gave physical, emotional, and spiritual 'rest' to many on the 'day of rest'. As he laid down His life He cried *"Finished"*[116] and rested from all His works having fulfilled all Scripture and completed all that was necessary for salvation for the world of men and women. He was also buried on the Sabbath day. Scripture is so careful to record it: *"that the bodies should not remain upon the cross on the sabbath day"*;[117] *"In the end of the sabbath, as it began to dawn toward the first day of the week."*[118] Is this why God rested on the seventh day from the work of creation? Evidently this day was when the Lord Jesus rested having completed the work of redemption - a day when angels fell silent. The incarnate Son of God was dead and lay in perfect

---

[114]Leviticus 24.8: "Every sabbath he shall set it in order before the LORD continually, being taken from the children of Israel by an everlasting covenant";

Numbers 28.9: "And on the sabbath day two lambs of the first year without spot, and two tenth deals of flour for a meat offering, mingled with oil, and the drink offering thereof."

[115]Matthew 12.8

[116]John 19.30

[117]John 19.31

[118]Matthew 28.1

holiness, resting in a borrowed tomb on earth. This day was the day when He demonstrated that He was dead and that He would shortly defeat death! No wonder the Sabbath will be remembered in a future millennial kingdom on earth when Christ shall reign[119]. Let us never forget the unique death, burial, and resurrection of the Lord Jesus.

Finally, prophetically, the Sabbath speaks of a future Sabbath rest on earth. This world that currently groans and sighs[120] will sing[121] when the jubilee trumpet will sound and the King of Kings will reign over earth[122].

In the light of these five purposes we can now understand some of the reasons why, at the outset of our Bible, God instructs us to obey the fourth commandment: **"Remember the sabbath day, to keep it holy"**.

---

[119]Isaiah 66.23: "And it shall come to pass, that from one new moon to another, and from one sabbath to another, shall all flesh come to worship before me, saith the LORD";

Ezekiel 46.1: "Thus saith the Lord GOD; The gate of the inner court that looketh toward the east shall be shut the six working days; but on the sabbath it shall be opened, and in the day of the new moon it shall be opened."

Rev.20.4: "And I saw thrones, and they sat upon them, and judgment was given unto them: and I saw the souls of them that were beheaded for the witness of Jesus, and for the word of God, and which had not worshipped the beast, neither his image, neither had received his mark upon their foreheads, or in their hands; and they lived and reigned with Christ a thousand years."

[120]Romans 8.22: "For we know that the whole creation groaneth and travaileth in pain together until now."

[121]Isaiah 55.12: "For ye shall go out with joy, and be led forth with peace: the mountains and the hills shall break forth before you into singing, and all the trees of the field shall clap their hands."

[122]Isaiah 32.1: "Behold, a king shall reign in righteousness, and princes shall rule in judgment.";

Rev. 19.16: "And he hath on his vesture and on his thigh a name written, KING OF KINGS, AND LORD OF LORDS";

Rev. 20.4: "and they lived and reigned with Christ a thousand years."

Notes

Notes

Commandment 5

Honour Thy Father And Thy Mother

"Honour thy father and thy mother: that thy days may be long upon the land which the LORD thy God giveth thee."

Exodus 20.12

Attribute: Stability of God
Principle: Regard for the Order of God

God is good. God is a God of fellowship. He knows what is best for us, society, and our relationship with Him. He created the family, and it is important to Him.

This fifth commandment, which is quoted six times in the New Testament[123], rightly belongs to the first table of the law that relates to our responsibilities to God. In honouring our parents, we are honouring God. In breaking up families and the authority of the home, Satan has removed the honour of God and the stability that underpins society. He has also removed the means whereby the values in the second table of the law (honesty, purity, trust, respect for life, contentment) can be upheld.

---

[123]Matthew 15.4; 19.19; Mark 7.10; 10.19; Luke 18.20; Eph. 6.2.

How we must pray for our nation today! Satan has relentlessly attacked the family unit. It was always God's intention that children should be raised in a stable, loving home. Increasingly, this ideal has been put to one side with disastrous consequences in society as a result.

Those of us who are parents must take our responsibility most seriously. God has delegated His authority and honour to families. Our children see us for what we really are. Do they see our devotion to Christ? We can stand out by merely ensuring that we walk according to Scripture[124]. A happy, loving, well-disciplined home where Christ is at the centre, glorifies God.

Raising a family, however, is also a very difficult task. There is pressure upon Christian parents to conform to the current thinking, and tensions exist around what should be permitted or denied and where lines should be drawn as we seek to keep our children from worldly associations. A good start is to revolve our family life around the assembly of God, just as Israel's life revolved around the Tabernacle[125]. Ensuring that the Scriptures are at the centre of our home is another sure foundation[126]. Praying together as a couple and as a family is vital[127].

Discipline in the home is essential. The word is not popular today. Proverbs says, *"There is a generation that curseth their father, and doth not bless their mother"*[128]. Paul, in Romans, says that the consequences of an anti-God state will be *"backbiters, haters of*

---

[124]Ephesians 6.4: "And, ye fathers, provoke not your children to wrath: but bring them up in the nurture and admonition of the Lord."

[125]Numbers 2

[126]2 Timothy 3.15: "And that from a child thou hast known the holy scriptures, which are able to make thee wise unto salvation through faith which is in Christ Jesus."

[127]1 Peter 3.7: "that your prayers be not hindered."

God, despiteful, proud, boasters, inventors of evil things, disobedient to parents"[129]. Is this not a good description of the western world today? This fifth commandment, however, was binding unto death[130]. The law in the home has great authority.

The principle for the believer is that our home is the training ground for God[131]. The brother who cannot ensure order in his house is not fit to ensure order in God's House[132], nor to serve publicly[133]. Having said this, the punishment of this law was against the son or daughter and not against their parents[134]. We should not be too hard on the Lord's people when their family go astray – our family might be next! Caring Christians dare not interfere with the discipline in another home (this is a sure way to create unnecessary tension!) but we can pray for Christian parents in this difficult task and help where it is practical[135]. What this law does highlight, though, is the need for authority in the home.

---

[128]Proverbs 30.11

[129]Romans 1.30

[130]Exodus 21.15,17; Deuteronomy 21.18

[131]Proverbs 22.6: "Train up a child in the way he should go: and when he is old, he will not depart from it."

[132]1Timothy 3.4-5: "One that ruleth well his own house, having his children in subjection with all gravity; (For if a man know not how to rule his own house, how shall he take care of the church of God?)"

[133]1 Timothy 3.12: "Let the deacons be the husbands of one wife, ruling their children and their own houses well."

[134]Deuteronomy 21.18

[135]Titus 2.4-5: "That they may teach the young women to be sober, to love their husbands, to love their children, to be discreet, chaste, keepers at home, good, obedient to their own husbands, that the word of God be not blasphemed."

The Lord Jesus honoured His Father. He did His will, spoke His words, did His works, and drank His cup. The Lord Jesus honoured His mother. On the cross He had said *"Father, forgive them"*[136] but before He said, *"Father, into thy hands I commend my spirit"*[137], He said, *"Woman, behold thy son!"* and to the disciple John, *"Behold thy mother!"*.[138] Wonderful love - even in the extremity of Calvary He did not forget the lonely heart that had lost everything. These words and those thoughts are in the eternal record to remind us that Christ honoured His mother. As the Proverbs say: *"Hearken unto thy father that begat thee, and despise not thy mother when she is old."*[139] We have a responsibility to honour our parents in old age[140] - a subject not popular today.

Obeying this fifth command will ensure *"that thy days may be long upon the land."* Israel would be reminded that their inheritance was contingent upon obedience. Ultimately their disobedience resulted in God removing them from the land. Obedience would mean their days were "prolonged"[141]. The life of the youth in Deuteronomy 21.18 came to a premature end due to disobedience in this commandment. We feel there is a general principle here that obedient, deferential, and unselfish living is

---

[136]Luke 23.34

[137]Luke 23.46

[138]John 19.26-27

[139]Proverbs 23.22

[140]1 Timothy 5.8: "But if any provide not for his own, and specially for those of his own house, he hath denied the faith, and is worse than an infidel."

[141]Deuteronomy 5.16: "Honour thy father and thy mother, as the LORD thy God hath commanded thee; that thy days may be prolonged, and that it may go well with thee, in the land which the LORD thy God giveth thee."

good for us physically, mentally, and spiritually. It has nothing to do with the fact that often the best of believers have been taken at an early age, but it does mean that the direct result of disobeying this command will bring *many sorrows*.

End times are associated with the breaking of this commandment. Selfishness and *"lovers of their own selves"* is listed along with *"disobedient to parents"* in eighteen sins prevalent at the end times described in 2 Timothy chapter 3[142]. The devil wants to destroy marriage, the role of a husband and wife, and the family unit. May God give every Christian child the desire to obey the Word of God: *"Children, obey your **parents** in all things: for this is well pleasing unto the Lord"*[143].

This commandment affects our relationship with God as well as our family. It is the only commandment with the promise of blessings for obedience[144]. May God give us help to heed the fifth command: **"Honour thy father and thy mother that thy days may be long upon the land which the LORD thy God giveth thee."**

---

[142]2 Timothy 3.2

[143]Colossians 3.20

Ephesians 6.1: "Children, obey your parents in the Lord: for this is right."
[144]Ephesians 6.2-3 "Honour thy father and mother; (which is the first commandment with promise;) That it may be well with thee, and thou mayest live long on the earth."

Notes

Notes

_____

_____

_____

_____

_____

_____

_____

_____

_____

_____

_____

Commandment 6

"Thou Shalt Not Kill."

Exodus 20.13

Principle: Respect for life
Value: Life

God values life. This sixth commandment utterly outlaws murder - intentional, causeless killing. God alone can kill and make alive. Hannah said, *"The LORD killeth, and maketh alive: he bringeth down to the grave, and bringeth up"*[145]. The sovereignty of life and death belongs to Him. Murder usurps God's authority. The punishment for murder was the death sentence[146]. This may seem like a paradox, but God authorised that a murderer should be slain. Those who cruelly take life in cold blood forfeited their own life. He also instructed Israel to kill the Amorites and Canaanites. God warned them over a space of 400 years to repent before commanding this execution[147]. The reason is that they had been

---

[145]1 Samuel 2.6

[146]Deuteronomy 19.11-13; Romans 13.4

[147]Genesis 15.13-16: "And he said unto Abram, Know of a surety that thy seed shall be a stranger in a land that is not theirs, and shall serve them; and they shall afflict them four hundred years; And also that nation, whom they shall serve, will I judge: and afterward shall they come out with great substance. And thou shalt go to thy fathers in peace; thou

guilty of infanticide, murdering their own children in a ritual to Molech their god[148]. They had also been guilty of many utterly vile and unmentionable sexual sins[149], some of them listed in Leviticus 18 and 20. God in His sovereignty used Israel as a vehicle to destroy these murderers[150]. Hebrew law recognised

---

shalt be buried in a good old age. But in the fourth generation they shall come hither again: for the iniquity of the Amorites is not yet full."

[148]Leviticus 18.21; "And thou shalt not let any of thy seed pass through the fire to Molech, neither shalt thou profane the name of thy God: I *am* the LORD." See Leviticus 20.2.

[149]Leviticus 18.24-28; "Defile not ye yourselves in any of these things: for in all these the nations are defiled which I cast out before you: And the land is defiled: therefore I do visit the iniquity thereof upon it, and the land itself vomiteth out her inhabitants. Ye shall therefore keep my statutes and my judgments, and shall not commit any of these abominations; neither any of your own nation, nor any stranger that sojourneth among you: (For all these abominations have the men of the land done, which were before you, and the land is defiled;) That the land spue not you out also, when ye defile it, as it spued out the nations that were before you." See also Leviticus 18.3.

Leviticus 20.23: "And ye shall not walk in the manners of the nation, which I cast out before you: for they committed all these things, and therefore I abhorred them."

[150]Deuteronomy 9.5: "Not for thy righteousness, or for the uprightness of thine heart, dost thou go to possess their land: but for the wickedness of these nations the LORD thy God doth drive them out from before thee, and that he may perform the word which the LORD sware unto thy fathers, Abraham, Isaac, and Jacob";

See Deuteronomy 12.2;

Deu. 18.9: "When thou art come into the land which the LORD thy God giveth thee, thou shalt not learn to do after the abominations of those nations";

See Deu.18.14

accidental killing as differing from murder. Specific towns (cities of refuge) were designated to which unintentional killers could flee to escape retribution[151].

Homicide

The sin of murder is wrong. Taking another person's life is explicitly outlawed in the Bible on another seven occasions[152]. It is also one of seven deadly sins listed in Matthew 15[153]. It was broken by the first man born into the world – Cain. He was followed quickly by Lamech and millions since. The days before the flood were *"filled with violence"*[154]. The days before the final judgment will be the same[155]. We live in an increasingly violent world. Knife crime is rife in many of our major world cities and towns. Gun crime is now common in the western world. Acts of terrorism have become more extreme and violent in the last decade with almost weekly reports of bombings, beheadings and lorries being driven at full speed into crowds of people, killing and destroying many lives. Truly the judgment of this world cannot now be long[156].

---

[151]Numbers 35.11: "Then ye shall appoint you cities to be cities of refuge for you; that the slayer may flee thither, which killeth any person at unawares."

[152]Deu. 5.17; Matt. 5.21, 19.18; Mk. 10.19; Lk. 18.20; Rom. 13.9; Jas. 2.11

[153]Matt. 15.19: "For out of the heart proceed evil thoughts, murders, adulteries, fornications, thefts, false witness, blasphemies."

[154]Genesis 6.11: "The earth also was corrupt before God, and the earth was filled with violence."

[155]2 Timothy 3.1-14

[156]Acts 17.31: "Because he hath appointed a day, in the which he will judge the world in righteousness by *that* man whom he hath ordained; *whereof* he hath given assurance unto all *men*, in that he hath raised him from the dead."

Abortion

In the UK, every three years, the lives of a large city of small unborn children (600,000 souls) are ended medically[157]. The Bible is clear that life begins in the womb at conception[158]. God gives the power to conceive seed[159]. A country that once prided itself in its honour of God and sent out thousands of missionaries to other countries with the Gospel of Christ is now guilty of millions of cases of infanticide. We do realise that there can be times when medically, it is very difficult to know what to do, and significant ethical issues can be raised for doctors, for example separating

---

[157]Report on abortion statistics in England and Wales for 2015: Department of Health, Abortion statistics, England and Wales, 17 May 2016.

[158]Isaiah 44.2: "Thus saith the LORD that made thee, and formed thee from the womb";

Isaiah 49.1: "The LORD hath called me from the womb";

Psalm 139.13-18: "For thou hast possessed my reins: thou hast covered me in my mother's womb. I will praise thee; for I am fearfully and wonderfully made: marvellous are thy works; and that my soul knoweth right well. My substance was not hid from thee, when I was made in secret, and curiously wrought in the lowest parts of the earth. Thine eyes did see my substance, yet being unperfect; and in thy book all my members were written, which in continuance were fashioned, when as yet there was none of them. How precious also are thy thoughts unto me, O God! how great is the sum of them!"

[159]Gen 16.2: "And Sarai said unto Abram, Behold now, the LORD hath restrained me from bearing."

Gen 29.31: "And when the LORD saw that Leah *was* hated, he opened her womb";

Gen. 30.2: "And Jacob's anger was kindled against Rachel: and he said, *Am* I in God's stead, who hath withheld from thee the fruit of the womb?"

Gen. 30.22: "And God remembered Rachel, and God hearkened to her, and opened her womb."

Siamese twins. God knows all about this. Furthermore, it is often in cases of extremity that women seek abortion. Often the trauma and regret faced afterward lasts a lifetime. Nevertheless, society has legitimized something that is completely contrary to God's commandment.

Assisted suicide

We know that assisted suicide has now been legalised in several countries. People can arrange for a fatal injection to be administered when they wish to die. The trials of those who have a degenerative or terminal illness cannot be underestimated. However, the Bible is clear - humans have no authority to take a life. It is a clear breach of the sixth commandment.

Spiritual Murder

Many readers may well shudder to see this heading in sequence with the others listed above! However, it was the Lord who gave the true interpretation of this law[160]. It was He who said that murder starts in the heart and that unchecked anger against our brother is murder. We have three degrees of sin here in Matthew chapter 5.21-22:

(i) causeless anger
(ii) contempt and scorn for our brother [Raca]
(iii) fixed and settled hatred for our brother [Fool].

---

[160]Matthew 5.21- 22: "Ye have heard that it was said by them of old time, Thou shalt not kill; and whosoever shall kill shall be in danger of the judgment: But I say unto you, That whosoever is angry with his brother without a cause shall be in danger of the judgment: and whosoever shall say to his brother, Raca, shall be in danger of the council: but whosoever shall say, Thou fool, shall be in danger of hell fire."

We have three degrees of punishment described:

(i) 'judgment' – there may be a veiled reference to the Jews of the local courts of Deuteronomy 16.18 but clearly the Unseen Judge deals immediately and directly with offences which in His eyes are unjust.

(ii) 'Council/Sanhedrin' – offences of this kind are placed by our Lord on the same level as those which came before the Sanhedrin. This assembly of men that met in Herod's Temple had the power to stone and put to death physically, as in the case of Stephen[161].

(iii) 'Hell Fire/Gehenna' – this is a narrow gorge on the south of Jerusalem[162] speaking of the place of future punishment after death.

John grasped the Lord's ministry. He said, *"Whosoever hateth his brother is a murderer: and ye know that no murderer hath eternal life abiding in him"*[163]. What strong language! The repercussions of enmity amongst God's people are most serious. Have we forgotten about the importance of loving our brother[164]; of not wounding his conscience and causing him to perish[165]; of going after our wayward brother and saving him from spiritual death[166]?

---

[161] Acts 6.12; 7.58

[162] Joshua 15.8

[163] 1 John 3.15

[164] 1 John 3.14: "We know that we have passed from death unto life, because we love the brethren. He that loveth not *his* brother abideth in death."

[165] 1 Corinthians 8.11-13: "And through thy knowledge shall the weak brother perish, for whom Christ died? But when ye sin so against the brethren, and wound their weak conscience, ye sin against Christ. Wherefore, if meat make my brother to offend, I will eat no flesh while the world standeth, lest I make my brother to offend."

The Lord Jesus was the one who was the *"prince of life"* and yet chose to die for sinful, undeserving humans like us. Many assemblies of God's people need to read this sixth commandment again thoughtfully and prayerfully. Perhaps the lack of blessing amongst God's people is because they have broken the sixth commandment and failed to act like Christ in love one toward another.

Let us never forget the significance of the sixth commandment, **"Thou shalt not kill."**

---

[166]James 5.20: "Let him know, that he which converteth the sinner from the error of his way shall save a soul from death, and shall hide a multitude of sins."

Notes

Notes

Commandment 7

"Thou Shalt Not Commit Adultery."

Exodus 20.14

Principle: Respect for marriage
Value: Purity

Adultery is infidelity within the marriage bond. It is no longer a shame to speak of this sin in many parts of the world. In fact, it is not only accepted but also expected in some quarters. "Affairs" are spoken of in terms of sensual excitement but not sin. We believe most people disapprove but it is still taboo to openly judge these matters. We forget that God is watching. *"Whoremongers and adulterers God will judge"*[167] is the solemn word of Scripture. Under 'the law', the sin of adultery brought about the death sentence[168]. James seems to suggest that adultery is worse than murder given the order of his words in chapter 2 verse 11[169].

---

[167]Hebrews 13. 4

[168]Leviticus 20.10; "And the man that committeth adultery with another man's wife, even he that committeth adultery with his neighbour's wife, the adulterer and the adulteress shall surely be put to death."

[169]James 2.11: "For he that said, Do not commit adultery, said also, Do not kill. Now if thou commit no adultery, yet if thou kill, thou art become a transgressor of the law";

Proverbs 6.32: "But whoso committeth adultery with a woman lacketh understanding: he that doeth it destroyeth his own soul."

"The way of transgressors is hard"[170] is the warning of Scripture. Adultery brings untold harm to individuals and the collateral damage extends beyond the spouse affected, to children, extended families, and friends. Could it be that due to the high prevalence of this sin we, as believers, have imbibed the world's view of this sin and forgotten how holy God is?

Of course, the Lord Jesus in explaining this law went further than the physical act of adultery. He made it clear that there was also a moral aspect to adultery that was intolerable to Him. *"But I say unto you, That whosoever looketh on a woman to lust after her hath committed adultery with her already in his heart"*[171]. Everyone must lower their head here. The Lord Jesus made it clear that His people must live to a higher standard than demanded by law. Indeed, to honour Him they must be prepared to pluck out their eye if it was a problem[172]. This is an example of hyperbole to make the point that sin is very serious and we must be prepared to make huge sacrifices or it will have eternal consequences. It is for this reason that many Christians guard carefully what they allow in their homes and avoid places where they know they will experience temptation. The media beams filth into the minds of humans daily, portraying men/woman as objects of desire. We are not immune from this. We must seek to live a life separated from its pernicious influence and pray for help to cleanse our minds from all the impurity in the world and the desires of the flesh. Joseph chose to be jailed rather than give in to the advances of Potiphar's wife[173]. What about us? What sacrifices have we made?

---

[170]Proverbs 13.15

[171]Matthew 5.28

[172]Matthew 5.29

[173]Genesis 39

The believing husband is instructed to be *"ravished always"*[174] with his wife's love and to love her *"as Christ loved the Church"*[175]. The believing wife is commanded in Scripture to *"love her husband*[176]*."* The world looking on should see Christian marriage as the ideal where both partners display loyalty and affection. If the woman is unsaved, the saved husband must remain loyal to her[177]. Similarly, the believing wife who has an unsaved husband is to remain loyal to him[178]. The possibility of separation is found in these verses if the unbelieving spouse is determined to leave, but this would not be the desire of the believing spouse. For some women in domestic abuse situations this may, however, be the safest course of action as *"God has called us to peace"*![179]. How we need compassion and help to support those in these dreadful and traumatic situations. What is never envisaged, however, is the saved husband divorcing his unsaved wife and remarrying whilst she is still alive. He still has a wife. This action is expressly forbidden: *"let not the husband put away his wife"*[180]. The point of all of this is to show to the world the importance of fidelity within marriage.

---

[174]Proverbs 5.19

[175]Ephesians 5.25

[176]Titus 2.4

[177]1 Cor. 7.12: "If any brother hath a wife that believeth not, and she be pleased to dwell with him, let him not put her away."

[178]1 Cor 7.13-14: "And the woman which hath an husband that believeth not, and if he be pleased to dwell with her, let her not leave him. For the unbelieving husband is sanctified by the wife, and the unbelieving wife is sanctified by the husband: else were your children unclean; but now are they holy."

[179]1 Cor. 7.15

[180]1 Cor. 7.11: "But and if she depart, let her remain unmarried, or be reconciled to her husband: and let not the husband put away his wife."

The Lord Jesus' teaching on this issue is plain and very different from the standards that we see around us today, *"Whosoever shall put away his wife, and marry another, committeth adultery against her. And if a woman shall put away her husband, and be married to another, she committeth adultery"*[181]. This is repeated in Luke[182] and substantiated further in the Epistle to the Romans[183]. In other words, the Lord could see no terms for divorce and remarriage at all; to do so would be adultery.

This is true of all legitimate marriages whether before or after salvation, otherwise God could never charge an unsaved man with adultery. This matter has only become a problem to many Christians in the last 50 years as it does not allow them to accommodate what is now standard practice in the western world. Sadly, this is another example of us lowering our standards to accommodate a world-view of sin.

It might be argued that many would not know what they were doing in unsaved days. Indeed! Until we are awakened to our need then we will never understand the gravity of some of the

---

[181]Mark 10.11-12

[182]Luke 16.18: "Whosoever putteth away his wife, and marrieth another, committeth adultery: and whosoever marrieth her that is put away from *her* husband committeth adultery."

[183]Romans 7.1-3: "Know ye not, brethren, (for I speak to them that know the law,) how that the law hath dominion over a man as long as he liveth? For the woman which hath an husband is bound by the law to her husband so long as he liveth; but if the husband be dead, she is loosed from the law of her husband. So then if, while her husband liveth, she be married to another man, she shall be called an adulteress: but if her husband be dead, she is free from that law; so that she is no adulteress, though she be married to another man."

sins that we committed in our unsaved days. Calvary removes the punishment and the guilt for sin but not the responsibility for past actions. Paul says of believers in assembly fellowship in Corinth who had practised these sins when unsaved *"such were (not are) some of you"*[184]. A thief who is converted has a responsibility to restore the stolen goods to their rightful owner. Equally the sin of adultery carries with it responsibilities. An adulterer has a responsibility to separate him or herself from continuing in the adulterous relationship after salvation, especially for assembly fellowship to be enjoyed. We must not be hard, and where children are involved, this can be extremely complicated. We say this with a great measure of Christian sympathy and sensitivity. Many of us are affected personally by these sins in our family lives. We are, however, quoting the Lord Himself. We know very well the enormity of the issues for couples and families. For those individuals hurt by an unfaithful spouse, the thought of remaining single for the rest of their lives is huge. However, the Lord always rewards faithfulness and His ways are best. *"Them that honour me I will honour"*[185] is the teaching of Scripture

If this teaching be regarded as a step too far for some Christians then let them reflect further on this seventh commandment in the light of the Lord's commentary upon it: "**Thou shalt not commit adultery**".

---

[184] 1 Cor.6.9-11 "Be not deceived: neither fornicators, nor idolaters, nor adulterers, nor effeminate, nor abusers of themselves with mankind, nor thieves, nor covetous, nor drunkards, nor revilers, nor extortioners, shall inherit the kingdom of God. And such were some of you: but ye are washed (or washed yourselves), but ye are sanctified, but ye are justified in the name of the Lord Jesus, and by the Spirit of our God."

[185] 1 Samuel 2.30

Notes

Notes

Commandment 8

"Thou Shalt Not Steal."

Exodus 20.15

Principle: Respect for another's belongings
Value: Honesty

Stealing is expressly forbidden in the eighth commandment of the law. Taking something that does not belong to you is wrong. This is hard wired into the human mind[186]. This commandment is expressly repeated on many occasions in Scripture[187]. Why should this law be emphasised so regularly? Why is it always in every list of commandments even when the commandments are partially quoted?

---

[186]Romans 2.14-15, 21: "For when the Gentiles, which have not the law, do by nature the things contained in the law, these, having not the law, are a law unto themselves: Which show the work of the law written in their hearts, their conscience also bearing witness, and their thoughts the mean while accusing or else excusing one another …. Thou therefore which teachest another, teachest thou not thyself? thou that preachest a man should not steal, dost thou steal?"

[187]Matthew 19.18: "He saith unto him, Which? Jesus said, Thou shalt do no murder, Thou shalt not commit adultery, Thou shalt not steal, Thou shalt not bear false witness";

Luke 18.20: "Thou knowest the commandments, Do not commit adultery, Do not kill, Do not steal, Do not bear false witness, Honour thy father and thy mother";

Possibly it is repeated because it has been broken by people since the dawn of time[188]. It was practised by the Ishmaelites, Chaldeans, Sabeans and the men of Shechem[189]. Robbers infested Judaea in our Lord's time[190]. Truth had *fallen in the streets* in Isaiah's time[191]. Has it not fallen in our times?

The Christian, of course, is exhorted to exhibit a different type of behaviour. An honest Christian life lived out before our families, neighbours and work colleagues is a testimony to Christ. The question could be asked, could a Christian steal? If there was no possibility of a Christian stealing then why would Paul exhort believers, *"Let him that stole steal no more"*[192]. Stealing may have been part of the former life before salvation but it was expected that salvation changed behaviour. Once Zacchaeus had met the Lord he said, *"If I have taken any thing from any man by false accusation, I restore him fourfold"*[193]. Could it be said of any Christian reader: *"Thou that preachest a man should not steal, dost thou steal"?*[194]

Romans 13.9: "For this, Thou shalt not commit adultery, Thou shalt not kill, Thou shalt not steal, Thou shalt not bear false witness, Thou shalt not covet; and if there be any other commandment, it is briefly comprehended in this saying, namely, Thou shalt love thy neighbour as thyself."

[188]Genesis 31.19: "And Laban went to shear his sheep: and Rachel had stolen the images that were her father's."

[189]Gen.16.12; Job 1.15, Job 1.17; Jdg.9.25.

[190]Luke 10.30; John 18.40; Acts 5.36-37.

[191]Isa.59.14: "And judgment is turned away backward, and justice standeth afar off: for truth is fallen in the street, and equity cannot enter."

[192]Ephesians 4.28

[193]Luke 19.8

[194]Romans 2.21

Stealing can be secretive. In Rachel's case, even her husband Jacob did not suspect it[195]. Sometimes it can be open robbery like the men of Shechem[196]. Whether public or private it is always wrong. Stealing can be a temptation, especially in times of poverty. The wise man prayed: *"Lest I be poor, and steal, and take the name of my God in vain[197]."* When completing the tax return for the government it would be easy to tell lies if the business or the home finances were stretched. We must never forget the watching eye of God. To steal is to take His Name in vain.

Stealing can be keeping something that has been loaned to you or that you have found and not returned to the owner. Leviticus teaches us that if *"we have found that which was lost, and lieth concerning it and sweareth falsely .... then it shall be ... that he shall restore that .... he hath deceitfully gotten, or that which was delivered him to keep, or the lost thing which he found, ... he shall even restore it in the principal, and shall add the fifth part more thereto"*[198]. Do we regard loans as gifts? The Bible demands confession, restoration, and even restitution.

Stealing can be ensuring that we extract the maximum amount and a little bit more from those who are weaker and unable to defend themselves. Often, we see this in the world. God will not hold that person guiltless. Christian businessmen must be careful

---

[195]Genesis 31.32: "With whomsoever thou findest thy gods, let him not live: before our brethren discern thou what is thine with me, and take it to thee. For Jacob knew not that Rachel had stolen them."

[196]Judges 9.25: "And the men of Shechem set liers in wait for him in the top of the mountains, and they robbed all that came along that way by them: and it was told Abimelech."

[197]Proverbs 30.9

[198]Leviticus 6.3-5

that their behaviour is different from their colleagues. Big bonuses for the top managers while at the same time squeezing the salary of the lowest paid workers should not be a feature of a Christian businessman. Proverbs teaches us, *"Rob not the poor, because he is poor: neither oppress the afflicted in the gate"*[199]. Isaiah condemns the people of his day who *"turn aside the needy from judgment.... take away the right from the poor of my people, ... that they may rob the fatherless!"*[200].

Stealing can be stealing God's words. If we claim originality for something in written or oral form that belongs to another then that is plagiarism. This is something that schools, colleges and university students are made aware of. Plagiarism is no less sin when committed in spiritual things. Those who preach or write books on Scripture need to be very careful. The Lord said, *"I am against the prophets, saith the LORD, that steal my words everyone from his neighbour"*[201]. Genuine mistakes can easily be made, and undoubtedly many of us will have inadvertently used another's words without due acknowledgement at the time. It is deliberately taking the words and ideas of another and claiming them personally, which would be wrong.

Perhaps the most serious form of stealing is stealing from God directly. Surely this would be worse than blatant robbery from men? Malachi asked this question, *"Will a man rob God?"* The answer came back: *"Yet ye have robbed me."* Israel said, *"Wherein have we robbed thee?"* The answer was, *"In tithes and offerings"*[202]. The brother or sister who has nothing to give in worship at the

---

[199]Proverbs 22.22

[200]Isaiah 10.2

[201]Jeremiah 23.30

[202]Malachi 3.8-9

Breaking of Bread is robbing God. The brother or sister who does not give God His due from their lives is in danger. We dare not keep back anything from God. It all belongs to Him.

Our blessed Lord came not to steal but to give[203]. He warned of the thief, and, paradoxically, the world crucified Him between two robbers. One day we will be with Him and be in a place where there is no fear of the thief or the robber[204]. As we meditate on the person of Christ, may we learn now the importance of this eighth commandment, **"Thou shalt not steal."**

---

[203]John 10.10: "The thief cometh not, but for to steal, and to kill, and to destroy: I am come that they might have life, and that they might have it more abundantly."

[204]Matthew 6.19-20: "Lay not up for yourselves treasures upon earth, where moth and rust doth corrupt, and where thieves break through and steal: But lay up for yourselves treasures in heaven, where neither moth nor rust doth corrupt, and where thieves do not break through nor steal."

Notes

Notes

Commandment 9

Thou Shalt Not Bear False Witness

"Thou shalt not bear false witness against thy neighbour."

Exodus 20.16

Principle: Respect for truth
Value: Trust

God is a God of truth and hates falsehood and lying. Interestingly, if there is one of the Ten Commandments that many seem to readily admit that they have broken it is this one – number 9. It seems strange that we can so publicly admit to lying without blushing. It is not as if the consequences of breaking this law are any different from any of the others. It is the second and sixth of the seven abominations[205]. The statements in Scripture are stark. *"A false witness shall not be unpunished"*[206] and *"he that speaketh lies shall perish"*[207]. Read Deuteronomy 19.16-19[208]!

---

[205]Proverbs 6.16-19: "These six things doth the LORD hate: yea, seven are an abomination unto him: A proud look, a lying tongue, and hands that shed innocent blood, An heart that deviseth wicked imaginations, feet that be swift in running to mischief, A false witness that speaketh lies, and he that soweth discord among brethren."

[206]Proverbs 19.5

[207]Proverbs 19.9

This commandment is not only for Old Testament saints. It is repeated four times in the New Testament[209]. The conditions of the human heart have not changed; it is one of the seven deadly sins spoken of by the Lord Jesus[210]. The consequences remain the same, in fact one of the most solemn chapters in the New Testament is Acts chapter 5 which outlines the death of a husband and wife who were struck down dead for lying to God.

The men of Job's day knew all about lying[211]. The prophets despaired in each generation that people told lies and did so in God's name: Isaiah[212], Jeremiah[213], Ezekiel[214], Hosea[215], Amos[216], Micah[217], Nahum[218], Habakkuk[219], and Zechariah[220]. This did not alter in the Apostle Paul's day when he spoke of those who would *"speak lies in hypocrisy; having their conscience seared with a hot iron"*[221]. Unfaithfulness marks our day, lying and a lack of trust. How different the Christian should be!

---

[208]Deuteronomy 19.16-19: "If a false witness rise up against any man to testify against him that which is wrong; Then both the men, between whom the controversy is, shall stand before the LORD, before the priests and the judges, which shall be in those days; And the judges shall make diligent inquisition: and, behold, if the witness be a false witness, and hath testified falsely against his brother; Then shall ye do unto him, as he had thought to have done unto his brother: so shalt thou put the evil away from among you."

[209]Matthew 19.18; Mark 10.19; Luke 18.20; Romans 13.9

[210]Matthew 15.19: "For out of the heart proceed evil thoughts, murders, adulteries, fornications, thefts, false witness, blasphemies".

[211]Job 11.3: "Should thy lies make men hold their peace? and when thou mockest, shall no man make thee ashamed?"

[212]Isaiah 59.4: "None calleth for justice, nor any pleadeth for truth: they trust in vanity, and speak lies; they conceive mischief, and bring forth iniquity."

Telling lies is an old sin first committed in the Garden of Eden by the evil one – *"the father of lies"*[222]. We were born into a race who followed in his ways. The believer, however, now has the power to follow the ways of the One who is the truth[223]. Indeed, we are instructed: *"Wherefore putting away lying, speak every man truth with his neighbour: for we are members one of another"*[224]. It is a serious sin for a Christian to tell lies about his neighbour. We should never excuse it. All who know us should testify that we tell the truth. The Psalmist prayed, *"Deliver my soul, O LORD, from lying lips, and from a deceitful tongue"*[225].

---

[213]Jer. 14.14: "Then the LORD said unto me, The prophets prophesy lies in my name: I sent them not, neither have I commanded them, neither spake unto them: they prophesy unto you a false vision and divination, and a thing of nought, and the deceit of their heart."

[214]Ezek. 22.28: "And her prophets have daubed them with untempered mortar, seeing vanity, and divining lies unto them, saying, Thus saith the Lord GOD, when the LORD hath not spoken."

[215]Hosea 11.12: "Ephraim compasseth me about with lies, and the house of Israel with deceit: but Judah yet ruleth with God, and is faithful with the saints."

[216]Amos 2.4: "Thus saith the LORD; For three transgressions of Judah, and for four, I will not turn away the punishment thereof; because they have despised the law of the LORD, and have not kept his commandments, and their lies caused them to err, after the which their fathers have walked"

[217]Micah 6.12: 'For the rich men thereof are full of violence, and the inhabitants thereof have spoken lies, and their tongue *is* deceitful in their mouth."

[218]Nahum 3.1: "Woe to the bloody city! it *is* all full of lies and robbery; the prey departeth not";

Sometimes our understanding of truth can be very limited. The Scriptures outline what telling lies can mean in practice; sometimes it may surprise the believer how liars are defined:

1. A liar can be someone who is disobedient to Christ: *"He that saith, I know him, and keepeth not his commandments, is a liar, and the truth is not in him"*[226].

2. A liar can also be someone who denies the sovereignty of

---

[219]Habakkuk 2.18: "What profiteth the graven image that the maker thereof hath graven it; the molten image, and a teacher of lies, that the maker of his work trusteth therein, to make dumb idols?"

[220]Zechariah 13.3: "And it shall come to pass, *that* when any shall yet prophesy, then his father and his mother that begat him shall say unto him, Thou shalt not live; for thou speakest lies in the name of the LORD: and his father and his mother that begat him shall thrust him through when he prophesieth."

[221]1 Timothy 4.2

[222]John 8.44

[223]Romans 6.16-19: "Know ye not, that to whom ye yield yourselves servants to obey, his servants ye are to whom ye obey; whether of sin unto death, or of obedience unto righteousness? But God be thanked, that ye were the servants of sin, but ye have obeyed from the heart that form of doctrine which was delivered you. Being then made free from sin, ye became the servants of righteousness. I speak after the manner of men because of the infirmity of your flesh: for as ye have yielded your members servants to uncleanness and to iniquity unto iniquity; even so now yield your members servants to righteousness unto holiness."

[224]Ephesians 4.25

[225]Psalm 120.2

[226]1 John 2.4

[227]1 John 2.22

[228]1 John 4.20

Christi: *"Who is a liar but he that denieth that Jesus is the Christ? He is antichrist, that denieth the Father and the Son"*[227].

3. A liar can be someone who does not love his brother: *"If a man say, I love God, and hateth his brother, he is a liar: for he that loveth not his brother whom he hath seen, how can he love God whom he hath not seen?"* [228].

4. A liar is someone who does not believe God: *"He that believeth on the Son of God hath the witness in himself: he that believeth not God hath made him a liar; because he believeth not the record that God gave of His Son"*[229].

It is statements like these that can challenge our understanding of truth and underscore how seriously God takes this matter.

---

[229]1 John 5.10

[230]John 14.6

[231]Matthew 5.34-37: "But I say unto you, Swear not at all; neither by heaven; for it is God's throne: Nor by the earth; for it is his footstool: neither by Jerusalem; for it is the city of the great King. Neither shalt thou swear by thy head, because thou canst not make one hair white or black. But let your communication be, Yea, yea; Nay, nay: for whatsoever is more than these cometh of evil."
2 Cor 1.17-20: "When I therefore was thus minded, did I use lightness? or the things that I purpose, do I purpose according to the flesh, that with me there should be yea yea, and nay nay? But as God is true, our word toward you was not yea and nay. For the Son of God, Jesus Christ, who was preached among you by us, even by me and Silvanus and Timotheus, was not yea and nay, but in him was yea. For all the promises of God in him are yea, and in him Amen, unto the glory of God by us."

The Lord Jesus is not only true but also the "truth"[230]. He warned against those who had to make an oath or swear before anyone would take them seriously. He wanted our "Yes" to mean "Yes" and our "No" to mean "No"[231]. The Lord Jesus is the *faithful witness*[232]. He had to endure false witnesses when He was here[233]. He would not expect His disciples to *"bear false witness against their neighbour"*. Is this the case? The Psalmist could say, *"I hate and abhor lying: but thy law do I love"*[234].

One day, this world will worship a man *"whose coming is after the working of Satan with all power and signs and lying wonders"*[235] and they will *"believe a lie"*. This is the antichrist, the Man of Sin. However, the power of the Man of Sin will be smashed by the One who rides on the white horse out of heaven and whose Name is *"Faithful and True"*[236], even our Lord Jesus Christ. It is a humbling thought that we are joined to such a Saviour. Let us never forget then His Name and seek to honour Him in obedience, honouring the ninth commandment: **"Thou shalt not bear false witness."**

---

[232]Revelation 1.5

[233]Matthew 26.59-61: "Now the chief priests, and elders, and all the council, sought false witness against Jesus, to put him to death; But found none: yea, though many false witnesses came, yet found they none. At the last came two false witnesses, And said, This fellow said, I am able to destroy the temple of God, and to build it in three days."

[234]Psalm 119.163

[235]2 Thessalonians 2.9,11

[236]Revelation 19.11

Notes

Notes

Commandment 10

Thou Shalt Not Covet

"Thou shalt not covet thy neighbour's house, thou shalt not covet thy neighbour's wife, nor his manservant, nor his maidservant, nor his ox, nor his ass, nor any thing that is thy neighbour's."

Exodus 20.17

Principle: Respect for what I have
Value: Contentment

To covet means to delight in; to count something precious or to set the heart upon something. It almost always means desiring something illicitly, but there are exceptions where it is used in a positive way[237]. However, this last and tenth commandment is saying that you shall not desire something that belongs to your neighbour, such as his wife, his lifestyle, his privileges, or his belongings.

The sin of coveting starts in the heart. This law brings it out into the open, for example, lusting after another man's wife. Paul says, *"Nay, I had not known sin, but by the law: for I had not known lust, except the law had said, Thou shalt not covet"*[238].

---

[237]1 Cor. 12.31; 14.39

[238]Romans 7.7

It was this law that the rich young ruler did not keep[239]. He maintained that he had kept all the commandments from "*his youth up*". But when he was tested on commandment number ten, he went away from the Lord sad. It was this sin that Achan failed in when he coveted the wedge of gold in Jericho with disastrous consequences[240]. It was the sin of covetousness that David failed in when he watched Bathsheba washing[241]. We do not need to remind the reader of the consequences of that action. This sin is serious.

Paul states that those who practise this sin habitually will not be in heaven[242]. Moreover, he also said that a covetous man could not be considered an elder in a local assembly[243]. This has not changed since the days of Exodus; the leaders then were men

---

[239]Matthew 19.16-23

[240]Joshua 7.21

[241]2 Samuel 12.10-12: "Now therefore the sword shall never depart from thine house; because thou hast despised me, and hast taken the wife of Uriah the Hittite to be thy wife. Thus saith the LORD, Behold, I will raise up evil against thee out of thine own house, and I will take thy wives before thine eyes, and give them unto thy neighbour, and he shall lie with thy wives in the sight of this sun. For thou didst it secretly: but I will do this thing before all Israel, and before the sun."

[242]1 Cor. 6.10-11: "Nor thieves, nor covetous, nor drunkards, nor revilers, nor extortioners, shall inherit the kingdom of God. And such were some of you: but ye are washed, but ye are sanctified, but ye are justified in the name of the Lord Jesus, and by the Spirit of our God"; Ephesians 5.5: "For this ye know, that no whoremonger, nor unclean person, nor covetous man, who is an idolater, hath any inheritance in the kingdom of Christ and of God."

[243]1 Tim 3.3: "Not given to wine, no striker, not greedy of filthy lucre; but patient, not a brawler, not covetous";

who *"hated covetousness"*[244]. Those who commit this sin must be removed from the assembly[245]. This is solemn.

This basic selfishness of illicit desire marks the world[246]. There is a danger that this "discontent" could spill over into Christian lives[247], souring life and spoiling our testimony for Christ. Religion,

---

[244]Exodus 18.21: "Moreover thou shalt provide out of all the people able men, such as fear God, men of truth, hating covetousness; and place such over them, to be rulers of thousands, and rulers of hundreds, rulers of fifties, and rulers of tens."

[245]1 Cor. 5.10-11: "Yet not altogether with the fornicators of this world, or with the covetous, or extortioners, or with idolaters; for then must ye needs go out of the world. But now I have written unto you not to keep company, if any man that is called a brother be a fornicator, or covetous, or an idolater, or a railer, or a drunkard, or an extortioner; with such an one no not to eat."

[246]Romans 1.29: "Being filled with all unrighteousness, fornication, wickedness, covetousness, maliciousness; full of envy, murder, debate, deceit, malignity; whisperers";
2 Timothy 3.2: "For men shall be lovers of their own selves, covetous, boasters, proud, blasphemers, disobedient to parents, unthankful, unholy";
2 Peter 2.14: "Having eyes full of adultery, and that cannot cease from sin; beguiling unstable souls: an heart they have exercised with covetous practices; cursed children."

[247]Ephesians 5.3: "But fornication, and all uncleanness, or covetousness, let it not be once named among you, as becometh saints";
Col. 3.5: "Mortify therefore your members which are upon the earth; fornication, uncleanness, inordinate affection, evil concupiscence, and covetousness, which is idolatry";
Hebrews 13.5: "Let your conversation be without covetousness; and be content with such things as ye have: for he hath said, I will never leave thee, nor forsake thee."

in general, is full of covetousness, particularly the desire for wealth[248]. This sin can affect us even if we are poor or rich. The Lord warned against it, *"Beware of covetousness: for a man's life consisteth not in the abundance of the things which he possesseth"*[249]. His life was the reverse of materialism. Paul was clear in this matter and went out of his way to emphasise it[250]. He warns Timothy of how it will snare many – particularly the love of money[251].

Covetousness is probably the biggest sin of our day. People are generally dissatisfied with what they have and materialism has a vice-like grip of their lives. Christians, however, should not be marked by discontentment, desiring things that do not belong to them, or outwardly needing to display their wealth or status. *"Godliness with contentment is great gain"*, says Paul[252]. We have an opportunity to show the world that we are different. We are taught to be *"content with such things as we have"*[253]. Before we buy

---

[248]2 Peter 2.3: "And through covetousness shall they with feigned words make merchandise of you: whose judgment now of a long time lingereth not, and their damnation slumbereth not."

[249]Luke 12.15

[250]Acts 20.33-35: "I have coveted no man's silver, or gold, or apparel. Yea, ye yourselves know, that these hands have ministered unto my necessities, and to them that were with me. I have shewed you all things, how that so labouring ye ought to support the weak, and to remember the words of the Lord Jesus, how he said, It is more blessed to give than to receive.";

1 Thess 2.5: "For neither at any time used we flattering words, as ye know, nor a cloke of covetousness; God is witness."

[251]1 Timothy 6.10: "For the love of money is the root of all evil: which while some coveted after, they have erred from the faith, and pierced themselves through with many sorrows."

[252]1 Timothy 6.6

[253]Hebrews 13.5

something, we should prayerfully ask, "Do I need this?" and take time to consider, "Why do I want this?". If our motives are pure, God will bless us. It is easy to desire the same things as the world and slip into so-called "comfortable Christianity" but this is so different to the radical teaching of the Lord Jesus.

In a world marked by individualism, selfishness, and a lack of care, driven by materialistic values, let us, as Christians, be different. The opposite of covetousness is compassion for others and a willingness to share what we have with others, for the glory of God. This is the spirit the Lord Jesus exemplified, One Who had everything and yet gave everything. Let us be vigilant, and by the help of the Holy Spirit, honour commandment number ten, *"Thou shalt not covet thy neighbour's house, thou shalt not covet thy neighbour's wife, nor his manservant, nor his maidservant, nor his ox, nor his ass, nor any thing that is thy neighbour's."*

Notes

Notes

Conclusion

We have come to the end of our meditations on the Ten Commandments. There is a summary of the Ten Commandments below. The first five commandments reflect our responsibility towards God, emphasising many attributes of God and principles that are essential in our relationship with God.

Commandment 1
Thou shalt have no other gods before Me
Attribute: Solitariness of God
Principle: Response to the Uniqueness of God

Commandment 2
Thou shalt not make any graven image
Attribute: Supremacy of God
Principle: Recognition of the Jealousy of God

Commandment 3
Thou shalt not take the name of the Lord thy God in vain
Attribute: Sovereignty of God
Principle: Reverence for the Name of God

Commandment 4
Remember the Sabbath day to keep it holy
Attribute: Sanctity of God
Principle: Respect for the Rest of God

Commandment 5

Honour thy Father and Mother

Attribute: Stability of God

Principle: Regard for the Order of God

The second set of five commandments relate to our attitude towards other people, stressing principles that are essential for harmonious human relationships and values for life.

Commandment 6

Thou shalt not kill

Principle: Respect for life

Value: Life

Commandment 7

Thou shalt not commit adultery

Principle: Respect for marriage

Value: Purity

Commandment 8

Thou shalt not steal

Principle: Respect for another's belongings

Value: Honesty

Commandment 9

Thou shalt not bear false witness

Principle: Respect for truth

Value: Trust

Commandment 10

Thou shalt not covet

Principle: Respect for what I have

Value: Contentment

The Ten Commandments were not only given to expose sin and underscore our need of salvation but also to reveal the glory of Christ. They were also given to be fulfilled in the life of the believer for their blessing in this life. It was the Lord who said that all of the Ten Commandments could be condensed down to our love for God and our neighbour[254]. He said the whole of the law and the prophets hang on this. Our love for Christ should motivate us to keep His commandments. The Lord Jesus said, *"If ye love me, keep my commandments"*[255]. Obedience to His Word will result in greater revelation, *"He that hath my commandments, and keepeth them, he it is that loveth me: and he that loveth me shall be loved of my Father, and I will love him, and will manifest myself to him."*[256]. It will also lead to greater intimacy with the Triune God[257]: *"Jesus answered and said unto him, If a man love me, he will keep my words: and my Father will love him, and we will come unto him, and make our abode with him."*

May God give us all help to treasure, obey and fulfil His commandments.

---

[254]Matthew 22.36-40: "Master, which is the great commandment in the law? Jesus said unto him, Thou shalt love the Lord thy God with all thy heart, and with all thy soul, and with all thy mind. This is the first and great commandment. And the second is like unto it, Thou shalt love thy neighbour as thyself. On these two commandments hang all the law and the prophets."

[255]John 14.15

[256]John 14.21

[257]John 14.23

Acknowledgements

The substance of these articles was written some years ago. The truth they contain is not new and is a mixture of our own personal studies, teaching by others in the assembly over many years, and help from written sources (see bibliography).

I would like to acknowledge the enormous debt I owe to my Father and Grandfather, Gordon and Kenneth Munro and friend, Edmund Ewan who all helped me considerably in my understanding of Holy Scripture. They are all now 'with Christ' but they lived out Christ practically, they remained true to their convictions and left a rich heritage to another generation. "Remember them who had the rule over you."

I would also like to thank my wife Hannah for all her encouragement and help with this book. Thanks too to my grown-up children Jack, Rhona and Edward for their constant support and patience. I would also like to thank Jack Hay for agreeing to write the foreword and for his careful editing of this book. Jack has been a source of real encouragement to me and I have often enjoyed preaching with him.

Bibliography

Brown, D., Fausset, A.R., Jamieson, R. 1961. *Commentary on the Whole Bible*. Grand Rapids: Zondervan Publishing House.

Coates, C. A. *An outline of the book of Exodus*. London: Stow Hill Bible and tract depot.

Meyer, F.B. 1978. *Devotional commentary on Exodus*. Grand Rapids: Kregel Publications.

Baxter, J Sidlaw. 1951. *Explore the Book*, Vol.1. London: Marshall, Morgan & Scott, 1951.

Grant, J. 2004. *What the Bible Teaches: Exodus*. Kilmarnock: John Ritchie Ltd.

Mackintosh, C.H. 1972. *Notes on the book of Exodus*. USA: Loizeaux Brothers, Inc.

Rawlinson G., Exodus. In *A Bible Commentary for English Readers*, (1) Ed C.J. Ellicott. London: Caswell and Company Limited.